The Pose of Happiness

THE POSE OF HAPPINESS

Poems by

GAIL MAZUR

David R. Godine

Publisher · Boston

First edition published in 1986 by
David R. Godine, Publisher, Inc.
Horticultural Hall
300 Massachusetts Avenue
Boston, Massachusetts 02115

Library of Congress Cataloging in Publication Data
Mazur, Gail.
The pose of happiness.
I. Title.
PS3563.A987P6 1986 811'.54 85-45963
ISBN 0-87923-615-9
ISBN 0-87923-616-7 (soft)

FIRST EDITION
Printed in the United States of America

for my father,

Manuel Beckwith

1911–1984

Acknowledgments

Acknowledgment is made to the following publications, where some of the poems in this book first appeared:

The Boston Review: "Dog Days, Sweet Everlasting"
The Hudson Review: "Mashpee, 1979," "Mashpee, 1952," "After the Fire," "Ruins," "Mashpee Wine," "Jewelweed"
The Little Balkans Review: "Listening to Baseball in the Car"
The New Republic: "Anomie," "Being Sick," "Reading Akhmatova"
Pequod: "Dutch Tulips" and "Pears"
Ploughshares: "Norumbega Park," "Hurricane Watch," "The Social Life of the Baboon," "Next Door," "Longfellow Park, August," "In the Garment District," "In the Dark Our Story," "Fallen Angels," "A Deck of Cards"
Poetry: "Spring Planting"
Prairie Schooner: "Early Winter," "Summer Rain"
The Seattle Review: "Pomegranate," "Teeth"
Shenandoah: "Daylight," "The Horizontal Man"
"St. Augustine, 1950" appeared in the Bulletin of The Poetry Society of America

Contents

1. *Mashpee Wine*

2.

3.

4.

·1· *Mashpee Wine*

Mashpee, 1979

The elements of the day aren't in accord:
warm sun on my hair, a blue spring sky,
the scorched holly and pines.

Where the low gray house stood,
nothing but metals and charred wood.

Better if it had vanished completely,
the fairy tale where I make one greedy wish
too many: *to have things just as they were*—

and then wake, stupefied,
to an empty space.

I can't say goodbye to this litter
of bricks, the twisted frigidaire,
our blackened bathtub
that sprawls in the foundation . . .

My parents stand by the rhododendron's
ghastly lace, showing the insurance detective
their few snapshots—

On the wide screenporch
overlooking the lake,
we hung Japanese lanterns one anniversary—

the picture shows five cousins, the picnic
table, candles flaming on the gaudy cake.

Mashpee, 1952

Dawn at the lake's edge.

In the glowing mist,
a lone fisherman—
my father—rowing in
with his catch of perch,
or pickerel, or nothing—

Or evenings, walking
in a headcloud of gnats,
the quiet road, blackberries
and wild roses, stars
waiting behind the mauve sky.

That summer, I grew into
a wide dimness, dreamt
of the family atom split,
a grandparent, or sister
leaving, never returning—

In August, we were cooled
by the lake's breath,
listened witlessly
to a blurred radio report
of Boston's heatwave.

And friends—long dead now—
mother's friends sprawled
gratefully on the porch,

reading easy Ellery Queens,
shades down in the rooms upstairs;

and the children,
lying on the porch floor,
pooling their decks
of playing cards, played
endless games of War . . .

After the Fire

I wake sometimes thinking, it's still there:
my father's red lumberjacket still hangs
on a hook in the back hall;

in the dining room, the veneer still
blisters and cracks on Aunt Belle's
upright piano. Dampness has made it
hopeless, forever out of tune;

a blue platter hangs above the mantel:
If music be the food of love, play on!
it orders us in blue calligraphy
around its unglazed border.

We were so unmusical.

Dumped in the country,
the old piano was usually ignored.
Once, my cousin, visiting
from his cheerful, sensible life,
groaned at the sound,

but that night he played us
his romantic repertoire—
Stranger in Paradise, I'm a Fool
to Want You, Tenderly—and we sang

off-key together
as Aunt Belle's piano,

getting the words
absolutely foolishly right . . .

That gleeful group of singers
must have been what my young parents
hoped for, buying a summer cottage
on the Cape right after the War . . .

As my cousin prodded the swollen keys,
the breeze moved up from the lake,
stirring the embers in the fireplace,
this deceptive flutter of my memory,

my family standing, joined
around the ruined instrument—

It wasn't music, really,
but we played on.

Ruins

The year my father bought the place,
a forest fire burned so close
it ate the outhouse, scorched the oaks.
We came, to explore the foundations
of cottages and old estates,
sit in the charred skeletons
of a tycoon's antique Fords.

Like scholars, we sifted the absent
neighbors' residue for souvenirs—
when I found Dutch iceskates,
I felt foreign, and fictional.

The damaged wilderness was ours
those brilliant dreamy week-ends.
My mother picked black-eyed Susans
and Queen Anne's lace for the table.

She dug a sassafrass tree
and replanted it in our yard.
We planned to make medicinal tea,
like the Wampanoags had brewed here,
from its green mitteny leaves.

That house held us so, we broke apart,
departed, one child following another
in a fury of independence—the family,
like milkweed in autumn, finally burst
from its pod and disappeared, scattered
to other locations, dislocations . . .

Now I cross the seared lawn
to join my parents; the arsonist
hovers here with an awful presence.
Mother, Father, what's ours in this
rubble? When they come to pick *us* over,
what will they find here, what did we leave?

Mashpee Wine

The barn still stands, but barely,
the roof's half gone, the walls
curve inward, windows slanting
without their panes. The wooden
floor has rotted; I can see
the hump of sandy dirt beneath it—
nothing left to save.

I tell the builder to tear it down.

The water tower, the pump house—
the house itself—have already
disappeared, their histories
undocumented, half-understood.

Years ago, when we brought
the tower down, we found it
littered with squirrel skeletons.
I used to bring my grandfather
tall, cold glasses of that water
as he sat in the sun, waiting.
"Mashpee wine," he called it.

Was it the drowned animals
that made it so delicious?

I'm nervous in the barn, afraid
today's the day it will cave in.
It's all shadows and a bit of light,
wind tears through the holes.
It smells of mildew, and worse.

Someone has dragged a damp
kingsize mattress to a concave
wall; beside the "bed," a 3-legged
chair (discarded from the vanished
kitchen), a sloping table;
the floor's been swept. A straw broom,
worn to a nub, leans at the former door.

The bed's so neatly arranged,
with matching sheets so neatly
tucked, I imagine hospital corners.
"The back seat of a car was good
enough for me," the builder laughs,
shaking his head—

but I think of these kids
so desperately domestic, snuggled
here in their fragile lair—love
isn't love without a place
to pretend to live. "The world
is a bridge," the Persians said,
"build no house upon it."

Tomorrow, this wreck comes down.

My father's given me the land.
To construct a house—to make
accommodations. . . . We walk out
to the scar that looks too small.
The porch goes here, I tell the man,
the kitchen over there. Up on the hill,
he drives the markers in.

·2·

Reading Akhmatova

This morning I went into the woods
to find a beech tree of my childhood.
Gray-limbed, motherly and capacious,
it once seemed to me the only place
to brood over my mournful lucky life.
It was still there, but leafless,
not much taller than myself. I leaned
my cheek on a cool dead branch
and stood that way a while until
my own mawkishness embarrassed me—
the way I always lament these small
inexorable shifts in the ecology.
So I walked down the hill, my feet
crunching in the dry beech leaves,
and swam in the old lake, holy
as the world's past. Only a family
of mallards was swimming there, moving
toward shore until they sensed me
and turned and glided away,
their feet making a frantic stir
under the water's surface.

I've lost no one.
Not my mother, alone today
under anaesthesia, my frail father
waiting here by the phone, my son
and daughter thousands of miles apart,
thousands from me. Last night I woke
again and again, heard my gray cat
scratching to get out, and kept him in.
I'm ordinary—my fears are ordinary.

Next Door

Snow trims the dead elm and the black
fire escape. Against the chill sky,
the red roof burns through a skim
of white. Bills and sympathy notes
accumulate behind the flat door.

The history of the house is hidden
to the eye—the alarm in the attic,
the glitter of a decade's argument.
Standing at my bedroom window,
I want to know nothing—

less than I know:
a woman loved a man, and other men.
The strange traffic of a world
coming apart. The blackness
that filled the rooms one night,
the sharp ring at the end.

We sat in the yard one summer
afternoon, calling over the fence
to a neighbor already dead.
A tiger cat miaowed at the door;
I caught and held her, wondering.

Now the cat's mine.

You're beside me here at the window,
shivering sympathetically. Together

we go over the details. We do it
until I recover. Each telling begins
my education again. I want to know
nothing less than I know.

Teeth

Where are my teeth?
my grandmother asks the room.
It's early Sunday afternoon;
her eyes explore the walls for reply.

She's asked four times today
in her new, thin voice.
Doc's been gone a year. That morning,
she heard pigeons at the window—
The doves were wooing all night,
she complained at the funeral home.
I wasn't sure she knew who died.

"Here they are," I answered every Sunday,
handing her the big black pocketbook.
She searches for dentures
and her change purse, pinned inside.

Reddish-blonde still, still almost
beautiful, she speaks fearfully
of coming here—*here* is our house,
or America—

At 17, she taught in a one-room
school in Maine, cramming each night
the math she'd never studied.
In a photograph, a dramatic portrait
from an amateur theatrical in Lincoln,
she was stylish, like a Gibson Girl.
American.

But she couldn't go on the stage:
it wasn't *nice*.

Where's my bag? she pleads
though it's in her lap.
Yesterday, she flushed a dollar bill
down the toilet. She meant to hide it.
She's forgotten that.

The stories she told are still intact:
the shaky escape from Vilna;
her courtships, inappropriate except for Doc
who had a dental practice;
her mother's stroke: great-grandmother
tried to smother the children—
my mother, my uncle—
to hide them from Boston's Cossacks.

But now she can't tell them anymore,
spilling her change in the living room.
She doesn't see the woman I become,
or see my girl—
who's going on the stage—
as she scrubs our copper roasting pan
brought over on the boat;

or my son,
who enters now, fresh from Jack's Joke Shop,
and opens a little red cardboard box
to show me a set of Chattering Teeth.
He turns a tiny key to wind them,
and off they go,
clacking mindlessly across the old oak table.

Fallen Angels

I almost died last night eating shrimp.
That's how they diagnosed it
at Mount Auburn Emergency after
they'd shot me full of adrenalin.
My heart fluttered, I couldn't keep
my hands still, and I laughed and cried
like a crazy person, my face swollen
with hives, my throat closing.

"I don't look like this,"
I insisted to an intern who
wasn't interested in my looks,
just whether I kept breathing.

Now everyone in the family's impaired.
Even my brother hears whistling
when he walks down his own hallway—
nowhere else. There aren't any windows,
so it's not the wind, and not tinnitus—
his ears only whistle in the one hallway.

We're used to his peculiar ailments;
he's our genius. Last year,
he was sure his face was falling.
And before that, for months he couldn't
read, or see in his microscope.
He thought his nose was beginning
to block his vision. An ophthalmologist
at the Health Plan said his eyes were
"normal."

We're what I used to call
"discombombulated."

To forget our troubles,
I go every night to a different *film noir.*
Sometimes my brother comes along.
We want to see a hapless loser
we can't identify with,
and some stylized violence—
Dana Andrews, grabbing women
too hard, and talking without moving
his thin, cruel lips; John Garfield
(before the blacklist), corrupted
because he grows up on the Lower East Side
and becomes a boxer and loves money.

We laugh dispassionately at Linda Darnell,
plump, coarse, contemptuous of men
as she pours coffee in a crummy diner—
Pop's Diner—every unattractive man
in town (population 4,000), including
Pop, slavering over the counter at her,
putting nickels in the jukebox
to play "Fallen Angel" again and again,
so the music's still going,
somewhere,
later when they find her dead.

Night after night,
I walk through the icy streets
of Cambridge, my home town,
the city I was born in. The neon
sign at the Holiday Inn is always

half-lit. In the bars, people
smoke cigarettes as if their lives
were a Fifties movie, and cancer
and coronaries couldn't afflict them.
Lucky for me
this town shows so many old movies.
I keep busy, work all day,
eat grains and vegetables, feed my cats,
swipe a sponge across the counters—
then, the entertainment. I know
there's something out there shady enough
to keep keeping me distracted.

Sunday Afternoon in the Asian Wing

My mother recognizes the Bodhisattva
Kuan Yin, known for her compassion,
by the lotus flower in her hand.
She stayed in an earthly life
because she was so sympathetic.

At seventy, Mother's a student again,
and still a teacher, like her mother,
like her daughter. I'm impatient
today with the Asian wing's serenity—
I need to learn impossible things,
all outside the mythologies of art.

Outside, the spring maples spread
their greenish branches over the fens,
and after a long week of rain,
residents kneel in the victory gardens,
planting tomatoes, squash and beans.

In the Forties, my father, too,
dug in his yard and planted,
joining our neighbors in patriotism,
his bad knee keeping him safely home.
Then, he wanted to go—

Turning over the rich, wormy soil
one Sunday, he found an old gold coin
he kept for luck. It glowed at night
on his bureau with the ordinary change.

Last year, when he lost it, he seemed
to fall from the List of the Blessed.

What my parents know they should tell me
now, not art history, but the names
of the wildflowers in our Cape woods,
and of the distant towns where our relatives
perished—our own history, that fragile body
that keeps diminishing, generation to generation.

Standing before the Merciful Bodhisattva,
I take my father's arm. I want to say
something that holds him here, to be a wall
that keeps him on my side of the world,
suffering world that Kuan Yin chose. . . .

Sunday after Sunday during the War,
when the backyard was all garden
from the clothesline to the river,
I watched him till and sow
those black, orderly rows,
afraid that without me, he might—
as my friends teased—
dig all the way to China.

In the Garment District

Nothing like 10 in the morning
for making love—cats glaring
from the table opposite, the dog
watching gloomily from the rug,

and after, opening cans
of their food, you in the shower
singing while elevators ring up
through the sidewalk, carrying
their racks of dresses, the noises
of ordinary business:
unloading, loading

Later, I stand at the window
watching a man in an office
through the arc of gold letters
that spells HESS REAL ESTATE.
He goes through his daily routine,
removes his brown jacket,
places it in a gray file drawer,
rolls up his sleeves.

And then, in the distinct light,
he stares down at the traffic.

He might, in his white shirt,
be wondering how to fill the day
but he's perfectly still. He might,
framed in the arched window, be part

of a Hopper painting, precise,
painful, not quite come to life—
the empty office, file drawers,
a bald man with nothing to do,
staring inward in the hard light . . .

And I know this memory of 20th Street
will come back often in the years
after we leave the city: bright sun
flooding the morning loft, you and I
loving, our animals arranged around us,
industry clanging on the sidewalk,
and across the street, a middle-aged man,
motionless, not quite anonymous.

In the Dark Our Story

is still unwinding.
It's 1919, the train's dropped us
in the Panhandle. This landscape
is only for the Farmer's pleasure.
We're stick figures, black things
moving in a sunlit picture.
How we love is our only secret.

The Farmer watches me hour on hour
from his velvet chair beside the field.
You say it's clear what he's thinking.
You say, *Marry him*, he'll die soon,
anyway.

What can I do—futility
burns in me in the blazing noons;
it's no blessing to be pretty
if it's impossible to be good.

I marry him.

He gives me everything—
a gilt piano, silk dresses,
pears served on a silver plate.
He gives me tenderness, and sometimes
the streaking sunsets make me
strangely happy.

Stuck with our plot,
I tell him you're my brother;

you move into the house to wait.
We three take meals together
on the sunporch; my husband
seems to be growing stronger.

Eyeing the rich wheat fields
we're dangerously lazy,
and together at table, nervy.
It can't last,
me loving you both, and defenseless.

Tonight he flies at you in rage—
over nothing really—your kissing me
in the gazebo; mightn't a brother do *that*?

I think when sound is re-invented,
someone will make a movie of this:
a soft-focus evening, the goldgrained air
turned ashes and black metal, hard knives
flashing, cutting our lives to pieces.

He couldn't touch me without touching me.

In the dark of my story,
you'll both be dead. This has to happen—
I can't signal the cameraman to stop.

All I know of passion is in the film
where I stand between you two,
afraid to move, and happy—

no, not *happy*, but in the pose of happiness
I've seen in pictures . . .

· 3 ·

A Deck of Cards

This chorus girl was pensive,
Sadness was on her brow,
Till she met her Sugar Daddy,
And she's ex-pensive now!
—from a Vargas queen of hearts

When Mister Mulryan called me into his office
to "show me something," I was lucky—
all he flashed was playing cards,
nude women in white cowboy hats,
one with a curving fishing rod and net.
I was eleven, no one could blame me
for confusing sleazy glamor and sex
and keeping it to myself, for finding
a goatish camera salesman romantic.

My father would have fired him
and avoided me for days.

At home, I took to the darkened den
and watched TV, old as I was
for Howdy Doody, and contemptuous
of Big Brother Bob who cursed one day
when he thought the microphone was off.
My father suffered, never to find me
waiting in the hall. The love I wanted
came late at night, after he'd left me
to lie in my spool bed, as my sister
in her spool bed slept the sleep

of someone still a child. Then I met
my 2-dimensional man, nasty in his cowboy hat
and spurs, dangerous with a dangling cigarette.

Only my grandfather saw me change,
watching from the hardship of retirement.
"Hedy Lamarr!" he called me, or "Veronica Lake!"
when my hair fell softly in my face.
Then I looked in the mirror and thought:
"*Pretty?*" I pretended headaches and sore throats,
stayed home from school, wandering voluptuously
from my bed to the overlit bathroom
where I preened with rouge and Shalimar perfume . . .

The next year I was taller
than half the boys in school.
Too awkward suddenly for baseball
with my brother's friends, I borrowed
a canoe and paddled on the Charles
to meet a destiny Thoreau had never
recognized. Sunk from the transcendental
mores of my favorite stories, I floated
on the dirty river, where toughs in rowboats
flirted across the waterlilies. Flattered,
ignorant, I paddled the term away.

In seventh grade, we traded dog-eared
books we didn't read but hid, and peeked at.
My Beginning Latin teacher confiscated one
from me, and blushed. I kept a diary
that Mother couldn't see . . .

Gallia est omnis divisa in tres partes.

I was divided, too—what use was Caesar?
I waited for my body's lines to curve,
remembering verses from Mulryan's deck
as I skipped home from school, mouthing
racy words, happy knowing everything is secret—
luscious secrets I'd never learn to keep.

St. Augustine, 1950

I'm the one on the left with the hair
parted in the middle, pulled tight
into barrettes; the little girl in pigtails
with three hats on her head, my sister;
my brother squints at the gate
of adolescence, dwarfed in his alpaca coat.

Mother tugs at my hair,
her back to my father's Kodak.
I'm already a head taller.
It's only the fourth day of the trip.

Early Sunday morning, we left in the black
Buick, snow heaped in record-breaking
drifts. The turnpike hasn't been built.
Or has it?

In Washington, the automatic windows
stuck, open, but we drove on into warmer
states. In the back seat, three of us
fought all day for breathing space.

This afternoon at Marineland, Jonny's watch
will slip from his skinny wrist
into the porpoise tank. This becomes
a family joke. He'll sulk through Miami,
two weeks of homework for a two-week vacation.

I sit on the sand writing "My Trip

to Florida" for my 5th grade teacher.
How clear this is, really, considering
the years the negatives lay in a drawer.
If only all pictures were this unclouded.

In front of the camera store on Mass. Ave.,
I sit double-parked, reassembling
the small square prints: the low stucco
building with shirt-sleeved workmen,

the palm trees, the Spanish entrance
to the park, tame flamingoes, Brownie
cameras dangling from the hands
of three pale children.

Being Sick

for Catherine Murphy

The pleasure in it diminishes.

Once, propped on fresh pillows
in my sunny bedroom, the yellow
flowered wallpaper, cats at my ankles
under the blankets, Ma Perkins
on the bedside radio, sounds
no one else I knew was hearing—
paradise was a mild virus.

Over six years of grammar school,
a whole year missed, at home.
Those one hundred-eighty days
should have earned me a malingering
prize at graduation. I'd wake
to the nostalgic soreness
in my throat, or head,
and could sink back into bed—

and the asthmatic nights in the country
when my father lit the fire,
put a kettle to steam on the logs,
and held me—*breathing*—on his lap
inside an army blanket tent.

To be sick, to be so loved . . .

Now the rewards diminish.

My face in the bathroom mirror,
ugly yellow smudges under my eyes,
reddened nose, memories of invalids
who didn't recover.

The cat prowls around my bed, unfed,
restless. A city plow burrows
up the frozen street, disabling
the cars. I should be up, working,
not watching an icicle
that cracks now at my window
and sinks into the snow.

Elementary Education

After recess, we file into the hall
in a Victory Stamp line, ready
to fight Hitler and Hirohito
with Standing Liberty quarters
and Mercury dimes. We stick
serrated squares into our books—
pictures of the Minute Man,
licked almost clean.

Then the art teacher arrives,
with her box of slimy plastolene.
Sitting crosslegged on the floor,
I roll fat pieces of clay
into snakes between my palms,
coiling eels to make a perfect bowl.

In the amber afternoon
of Miss McGreevy's classroom,
I think biography's the same as history,
and I plan my bowl's unearthing
years from now—*thirty*, maybe—
from my casket. I see my grown-up
dress, nail polish on my perfect oval nails.

I'll die of measles—
or a broken heart. A man who looks
like General MacArthur or the Father
of Our Country pushes past the family
at my grave and takes me away . . .

The art teacher's fragrance is different
from Miss McGreevy's or my mother's.
She lost her husband in the War.
Her fingernails are long, and painted black.

At the end of class, my bowl
will be an ashtray, or a loopy ball.
I forget—do I want to be an artist?
I can't think what I'd put inside the frame.
—I *won't* grow up to be a mother.

When I'm thirty, I'll be a famous painter—
silly to think anything else.

At two o'clock we write short stories.
I'm proud of my round obedient penmanship.
I announce, I'm going to be an author,
then dip my pen in the inkwell.

I'm a writer until the bell rings.

The Horizontal Man

Surely it was too awful to be real. The darkened library, the buildings full of empty classrooms, the threatening olive-green shape of the mailbox under the lamp at the centre of the campus . . .
—Helen Eustis, *The Horizontal Man,* 1946

On the second page,
my old professor's murdered with a poker.
His black curls, matting with blood
on the shabby rug,
were wild and gray
when he lectured to the Shakespeare class
on Sputnik and Ophelia. We'd all heard
of his affairs, and of this novel,
already out-of-print, written by a former wife

who killed him with a pen—revenge
more cruel than alimony
to young things on allowances . . .

When he recited "O, what a rogue
and peasant slave am I," we thrilled
to the alcoholic timbre of his brogue . . .

This reissued mystery
brings the whole semester back.
Fat, and pining for a boy,
I ate and smoked and slept most days away,
convinced I'd end up lonely, and alone.

For Professor F, I studied
"O that this too too solid flesh would melt,"
and earned the isolated A that failed
to keep my parents' hopes for me alive.

I recognize the Infirmary—
it's at the end of Paradise Road.
The demented freshman's dragged there
in the second chapter, babbling about love;
the nurse thinks she's the "perpetrator."

I remember the unwomanly physician
stricken by the vagaries of menstruation—
Is the psychiatrist from Springfield
the one they called the night my mind
was slipping, and the dean suspected
that wasn't all I'd lost that term?

In the spring nocturnes of my sophomore year,
I lay on my restricted cot,
confined to campus for my indiscretion—
my confession. I memorized soliloquies
for Doctor F—"To be or not"—
as if my life depended on my memory.
There was nothing I was going to *be* . . .

My teacher died, exhausted,
in a rest home late last year.

I've read all night again.
This *roman à clef*, with its bloody weapon
on the cover, is like the dream I stay up
to avoid, the classic college nightmare:

a gothic building, and months
of literature unread, the unversed girl

I never stop becoming, dragging
her cold feet through the scrollery
iron gate, past Paradise Pond
to the examination hall silently
filling with victims and perpetrators.

Jewelweed

We were talking about sex, taking
the dirt road to town, walking
slowly in the hot afternoon.

I hardly saw the fields
shimmering in the heat, the goldenrod's
itchy impressionist glow,

the pale touch-me-not,
or jewelweed, blooming in shade,
so skewed was my vision,

so interior. That day we agreed
never to touch each other,
passing the warm brown beds of pine

needles, the tiny graveyard. My face,
your face, reddened in August's ardent
flush; our hands clung to their pockets.

That conversation seemed harmless—
strange, that I still need
to put it this way—

Anyway, it must have been too far
to town. We turned back at a stone
marker to join our friends swimming

in a black pond deep in our past.
Now I am in the future where nothing
has happened, nothing happens.

What were we walking toward
that prickly summer day,
both of us suddenly guarded,

uneasy strangers, or greenhorns,
or children transported unprepared
to a heartless institution?

Pears

gone suddenly from the pear
tree, wrapped in tissue by the woman
next door, whose daughter never visits,
who'll give the fruit to her neighbors
finally, and some will be grateful
and some will shake their heads,
and a small boy will spit a piece
of pear on the sidewalk, hating
the skin, as the woman shuts the gate—

and I'll watch all this
from the window of my furnished room
this fall, conscious of my body,
and of my mother's pear tree,
the bushel baskets in the cool cellar
packed with tissue-wrapped pears,
and her own mother, blind,
frightened, not senile enough—

my grandmother, alone
in a tiny room in the nursing home,
waiting for her daughter's visits
which were daily and dutiful,
slipping in and out of sleep,
her scattered children, beautiful dead
sisters, her father the peddler,
and crazy mother, a huge dark boat
crossing the ocean, *the Old Country*,
copper pans, Sabbath candles
lit in brass candlesticks—

my grandmother, waking just once
at the end in her watery green room,
hearing her weeping daughter, saying
That's all right, I don't mind—

her words hum for a moment
in my cells, like the bees
homing in on the sweet rotting
fruit fallen by the pear tree
as the old woman, graceful in her
wasted giving, turns from the gate.

Early Winter

I wake in the rubble, not of war,
but an untended room. December.
The furnace is off.

Mornings, I taught my children
you rise and buckle your galoshes,
and face the world's great offerings.

I taught them as fast as I could,
barely holding my intelligence
a minute before passing it on.

After school, my boy played
in the warm kitchen afternoons,
cinnamon spicing the gloom.

I miss the simple expectation
of those days—departures
all followed by returns.

On the bedroom floor, a heartshaped
stone I took from the Sandwich beach
last summer. Gray and pink, cold,

it's the size and shape of my daughter's palm.

When you lose touch, I declare
to the grubby room, and then drift off,
not finishing my sentence.

Cold air, I'll learn to love you yet,
shake memory back to its place
so I can straighten up.

Memory, the last thing I'll put away.

Norumbega Park

A pink motel hovers over the river,
Shangri-la where local athletes
purchase local women in the lounge . . .
Is this where I grew up?

I paddle in my Oldtown canoe,
looking for relics of riverbank
that pre-date highway and turnpike.
Blackberries ripen by the black water,
a snapping turtle suns on a rock,
suspicious as his relatives, years ago.

In the Fifties, an amusement park
lured and lowered the neighborhood.
Summer nights, sucking in our breath,
we scraped under the chain-link fence
to Abbott & Costello and Boris Karloff
flickering in the mosquitoed dark.

The tumbling seats of the lindyloop
up-ended us until we were loose
with fright and shrieked to be let off.
None of us risked the rollercoaster,
or the two-headed boy,
or the man who ate live hens.

Freaks were like dead men—
we might be changed by seeing them.

We crouched and fed the ducks instead.

Or, invaded the Penny Arcade
for licorice and cotton candy
and postcards of the Hollywood stars.

Sticky and spent, I gathered Paramount
faces from the scuffed floor,
and brought John Hodiak and Lizabeth Scott
home to join Jeff Chandler
in a shoe box on the shelf.

I didn't know enough to save them;
they'd be collectors' items now.

Nobody saved the ballroom, its wine
velvet loveseats and gold brocade,
the carousel horses or the ferris wheel.
Or the moody brown bears
wandering in a limitless green field.

I watched them through barbed wire,
unnatural dangerous creatures
so resembling men they seemed
like coarse imposters, criminal.

But they were only unlucky animals,
out of place, like the brown mallard
who floats by me on the murky river,
her five ducklings swimming
secure in their artless childhoods.

November's Child

A few leaves cling to the ancient oaks.
Papery mums and zinnias fade in the annual gardens.
Not a choice month for a birthday—
for years, a great occasion of greed,
craving the undreamt-of present.

Now I relive birthdays in the house
on Longfellow Road—a *cul-de-sac*
near the hospital where I was born,
once a fragment of the poet's estate.
I thought I moved in widening circles away,
yet find myself again, today, on his sidewalk.
The yellow two-family houses make me lonely,
or less lonely . . .

Who knows what
a child wants? I had one party
at the Natural History Museum, now
a rose-bricked Bonwit Teller. Incurious,
I hankered for curios in the museum shop—
the petrified wood, sharks' teeth, glorious
peacock feathers—glowering at fossils
that weren't for sale.

They gave me a doll called November's Child,
said to be full of woe, although
in her gray velvet gown and bonnet,
she looked like the others, displayed
in a row on my shelf, unplayed with.

The differences were in the colors, the clothes;
May had the lace, green June the ribbons.

Today, I recall the gifts I didn't deserve,
and a package snatched back from me,
unopened, when I was rude. Again
and again, I've guessed what's in it—
a watch? a diary? a leafy silver pin?
a calligraphic pen I'd use now,

the virtuous daughter who preserves
everything, maybe too faithfully,
holding so hard to what happened,
what I didn't understand:
my greediness for whatever is withheld,
the mean bounty of November.

· 4 ·

Daylight

Sometimes the body loses faith
in the body. It's got nothing
to cling to then. Like the feeling
when you unlock the door
to your rooms, unsuspecting,
and notice the drawers not closed
quite right, and pulling them out—
yanking, really—you find all
the little jewelry boxes opened.

Grandpa's gold pocket watch,
a Chinese locket, jade earrings
you loved—all *gone*,
not having left the slightest
impression on their tiny cotton beds.

After a robbery, the physical
falls away. The detective tells you
there's nothing to wait for,
nothing will be recovered.
What's left must be spirit,
or the life of the mind—

or the will to turn outward,

to focus on the corporeal world
outside: a gray cat
in the neighbor's driveway stupidly
sniffing at a trembling squirrel,

the squirrel's bravura attempt
at escape—*Safe!*—
Kitty's tame confusion.

A small boy rides his tricycle
in circles on the broken sidewalk.
Blue morning glories scale
their taut white strings.
Someone drives off in a borrowed van,
the side windows painted, or decal-ed,
preposterous mauve and lemon sunsets;
one tail light's smashed.

Across the street, two dogs,
one black and white, one golden,
romp in the radiant abandoned lot.

Hurricane Watch

The power was off.
We cleared dishes from the table.
Shutters crashed against the windows.
Below us, in the lake, the minnows
were in a frenzy. Limbs cracked—
one great tree smashed to the ground.
Leaves flew past, pasted themselves
to the panes. Somewhere,
my father was on a train.

The blue walls quaked,
too weak to hold the roof up.
Telephone lines were dead.
We had no batteries for the radio.
Our neighbors weren't our friends—
we couldn't ask them for news.
We lit the charred wicks of the lamps
and watched the wind, and listened:
anything could crash and slide away.
Night passed crookedly like nightmare.

Wind blew in my chest.
We'd waited hours for father,
due home on the Beeliner.
Whatever mother feared, I feared.
Maybe the bridge was down.
I thought of the train twisted
off the rails; I couldn't think.
Kerosene glow from the neighbor's window

might have been stars glistening.
They didn't know we were in a frenzy.

I huddled tight in my bones
counting a million by twenties
to bring him home. In my mind,
the train was a Lionel toy,
anyone could smash it.
1000 . . . 1020 . . . 1040 . . .
At midnight the door flew open.
My dazzling father was home, with favors,
red swizzle sticks from the bar car.
I watched him hugging mother,
and heard the wind,
and kept counting.

Anomie

Gray morning and the first snow
spends itself at the sidewalk.
A man on a slate roof
clears leaves from gutters,
his visible breath
the calligraphy for *cold*.

Gray everything but his red jacket.

Quiet pervades the houses,
men and women at their offices,
children at school or still unborn.
The cats, left alone,
seek the mean warmth of radiators.

You, too, disappear into the day,
easy as opening a door—

Where would I want to go?
I board a bus where passengers
lose themselves in the tabloids,
their hands graying with newsprint.
Crimes of passion in Montana
stir my crazy yearning to confess.

I want to go nowhere: no counterfeit
paradise, palm tree at the patio edge.
No old European city demanding
I enter its museums and theaters.
No sultry nights on the savannah.

Black trees pass in a blur,
the Germanic Museum, the coin laundry,
the Home for Little Wanderers.
Snow thickens at the window
as we pull into the terminal,
the opening wedge into emptiness.

Dog Days, Sweet Everlasting

Weeks of ninety degree weather—
caniculares dies—
dog days, the Romans said,
certain Sirius the Dog Star
rose with the August sun
and added ferocity to heat.
I bathe every day in the lake
and listen for a rustle, a promise
of rain. A blue sailboat,
becalmed at the island, vibrates
in haze. Black quahog shells
gleam in the wild mint,
dropped there by glutted gulls.

I eat my lunch slowly
under a dark pine,
two tomatoes warm from the sun.

Languid life, writing at night
in damp silence; in the morning,
flopping down like a beached fish
at water's edge, the alewife minnows
and yellow perch swimming discreetly
around me, small bass hovering
darkly nearby in the dock's shade.

I want to live in natural secrecy
a while longer, to be unknown
to myself again, like the catbrier,

savage in its random scratchings—
or like sweet everlasting,
its bristly flower fragrant,
evanescent.

A hummingbird whirs and wavers
in the garden, choosing its honeyed
drink, cosmos or crimson bee
balm. And in an oak tree,
the catbird, clever mimic,
tries several dialects, hoping—
I'm sure it's what he hopes—
to find the song he's given to sing.

Summer Rain

for Jane

That morning on the island it rushed
toward you like a fervent family,
and it was so warm and you so suddenly
drenched in it, you stood laughing,
one of the children, your bag
of groceries disintegrating in your arms.

How old could you have been?
Ten years married, all your limbs
working like charms, although
the first shadow had already
fallen on an x-ray in the city . . .

All summer, you swam alone
in the sharp, nurturing surf,
your little dog dug into a hollow
in the sand. She never took
her eyes off you, she lived
for your return to shore.

It's August again.
The dog's buried in the backyard.
Your ashes are under the flowering quince.
I sit in my office watching the gray
sheets of rain. Three girls shriek
and take shelter in a doorway.

Remember, you took your sandals off
and danced along the wooden sidewalk
to the post office, the dog's fur
soaked to her body as she ran
frenzied circles around you.
Then, the bag broke, boxes and bottles
scattered, and the sun appeared,
its dateless promise
lavish and transitory as summer rain.

Longfellow Park, August

for Lloyd Schwartz

The day is so heavy movement
is nearly impossible; our clothes
stick to our thighs, to the granite
bench—a sweatiness without athletics
or the fever of intimacies.

Across from us, Miles Standish,
Evangeline, and Hiawatha
gaze blankly in *bas relief.*
There are others, too, characters
we're too dazed to name.

The pedestal which held
the bearded poet's bust is empty now,
scarred, a vandalism that's ancient history.
The great yellow mansion
that once stared down to the river
is obscured by maples, and developed lots.
There, his wife met her death by fire.

Those lives were not romances, either.

Afternoons like this leave us limp,
speaking so slowly in the sultriness,
as if the brain kept forgetting its task.
Disappointment emerges like a bruise, slowly,
and the desire to be cared for forever—

character, plot and incident formed
by a proper author.

Friend, we help each other when we can
but today we hide our stickier secrets.
Like *tics douloureux*, our faces ache
from the heat, from bafflement:
we can't revise anyone's life.

Dutch Tulips

The bulbs you smuggled home from Amsterdam
four years ago don't bloom this spring.
Last year, a few brilliant flowers—
perhaps two weeks from start to finish.

You spent your birthday at the Rijksmuseum.
In the damp November cold, I raked leaves
in a fury, digging my bare hands into the icy
piles, the dog shit fossils and dead insects.
I cursed you and our nearest neighbors
calmly bagging the shredded yellow waste.

When you called from Paris, I drove
charges through the transatlantic cable,
one grievance at least for each year
of marriage. Even to myself, I sounded
stupid and selfish. In a post office
phone booth in the *septième arrondissement*,
you were astonished, then hurt and silent.

Each separation then was a divorce,
a permanence I tested, rehearsal of loss
to try my strength. More than anything,
I feared being too domesticated.

I'm no different now.
I still don't forgive the bulbs,
forgive your travelling away.
Or our garden, flaunting
those cheerful inharmonious tulips,
flamboyant stamps on your passport.

The Social Life of the Baboon

He wonders why you keep postponing the party
when you have to do all the cooking.
One night, it rains for three weeks.
Brown water drips from the ceiling
and the *coq au vin* tastes like plaster.
His guests raise an eyebrow
and he wonders
why you don't just serve the *mousse*,
unflappable as *Vogue* at a party.

This time you're through,
you switch on the color TV:
somewhere near the Equator,
a woman studies chimpanzees
and they suck their thumbs,
showing off for the camera.
And high in the Virungas, another woman
follows the mountain gorillas,
gentle creatures playing
and nesting in the rain forest.

Apes aren't frightening on Educational TV.
Orangutangs and the others all look—nice.
Maybe that's the work for you, your true vocation.
You get hooked on the subject,
boring your man, alarming your analyst,
making your mother sick.
You have your appendix out,
pack the essentials
and book flight for the jungle.

Your family recedes.
You wash in a stream and none too often,
crouch by the hour with a little notebook,
by the week, the month, the year.
You're observing the quirks of your new set.
Happily, the beasts are curious about you, too.
Primates, you scribble, *are witty*.
They help you forget the city,
forget the life your mother planned for you,
your mate who declares you're loony
and marries a Total Woman;
they lead the social life he's longed for.

Bouncing in an old lorry across the savannah,
you fit coded notes into your book.
You feel so grateful to these vegetarians,
the vines, the rain, the Great River.
To television, which gave you
the first glimmer of your life.

You have no plans to leave.

Pomegranate

What I don't know about you could fill
a book, and probably will. We travel
circles around each other, and circle
this life together, too, unable to enter.

If I knew even a little magic,
maybe I'd press this pomegranate on you
and whisper to you in Oriental languages
of sacraments, and hopes.

Instead, I tell you how many centuries
the rind was used therapeutically,
that the ancients made a drug of it
to expel intestinal worms. I don't

have any idea what's inside you,
and though I bring you red orchards
of pomegranates and we spread the flesh-
covered seeds and try reading them,

I'd still need to travel pre-history
as if I were just drifting down Memory
Lane, to uncover the mystery—
how a woman remains underground so long

and yet returns
after eating "the fruit of the dead."

But what innocence would shatter,
what myth, if I toss you this—
this bitter medicine, my grenade?

Listening to Baseball in the Car

for James Tate

This morning I argued with a friend
about angels. I didn't believe
in his belief in them—I can't
believe they're not a metaphor.
Our argument, affectionate,
lacking in animus, went nowhere.
We promised to talk again soon.
Now, when I'm driving away
from Boston and the Red Sox
are losing, I hear the announcer
say, "No angels in the sky today"—
baseball-ese for *a cloudless afternoon*,
no shadows to help a man
who waits in the outfield
staring into the August sun.
Although I know the announcer's
not a rabbi or sage (no,
he's a sort of sage, disconsolate
philosopher of batting slumps
and injuries), still I scan
the pale blue sky through my
polarized windshield, fervently
hopeful for my fading team
and I feel something a little
foolish, a prayerful throbbing
in my throat and remember

being told years ago that men
are only little lower than
the angels. Floating ahead of me
at the Vermont border, I see
a few wispy horsemane clouds
which I quietly pray will drift
down to Fenway Park where
a demonic opponent has just
slammed another Red Sox pitch,
and the center fielder—call him Jim—
runs back, back, back,
looking heavenward,
and is shielded and doesn't lose
the white ball in the glare.

Two Months in the Country

for Joyce Peseroff

1

Dawn, and a mourning dove croons
its four notes over and over;
crows caw their harsh pleasures
near the overgrown raspberry beds;
aggressive as Saturday's cartoons,
the loud knock of a woodpecker—

a few identified calls and trills—
what earthly reasons to lie awake
so early in this room over the lake
where mists rise each morning,
and I wait for the day to burn off,

dazzled, as I used to be,
by the blue body, its soft
green shores, and three islands,
three mossy nests waiting
on the cerulean surface—
my lake, opening to me.

. . . But childhood never saw nature
as dazzling, not even the wild
roses, or Lady's Thumbs, not the waxy
Indian Pipes I found yesterday
in the dank woods—like scraps

of paper, or newly dead moths,
but growing, pushing out
through the brown pine needles.

When I was a child, I was told
not to pick or transplant them,
as if there were laws to forbid it.
Colorless as maggots,
they're ugly, morbid,
they felt—prehistoric.

Kingfisher, cormorant, nuthatch—
birds' names come to the tongue,
but my self-consciousness stays.

2

No one's written. The truth
is, I have no address.
Not to say I'm lost, or that
I "lose touch" with reality—

just too indifferent to sink
the heavy post for a mailbox
and learn a new postal etiquette,
the raised red flag . . .

But I have dreams again, thick
black Russian bread, thick white
butter, my grandfather upstairs
again, not dying, lying in a crank
bed, able to love the lake breeze . . .

When you visit, I'm wearing things
differently, raggy shorts, a torn blouse,
my hair wild sticks in the dampness.
I invite you in, but stiffly,

as if I were a hermit
in a tarpaper shed, ragweed
at my door, and enormous purple
thistles, brown spiders
moving on my books.
The sweet smell of honeysuckle,
not success.

Why am I here?
Why stay when loneliness
hollows me in the afternoons,
and at night, gnats, moths,
silent, distant constellations,
and I forget how to work,
except with my hands, in the dirt.

Graves

Mashpee

1.

Mornings, the lake's concealed
by mist. The Canada geese,
who lighted here this season,
are quiet now they've honked
through a wet starless night.

Alone, lazy to a point of stupor,
I think of wrecked vessels
on the Cape beaches, whose "bones,"
as Thoreau wrote, are still
visible jutting from the sand.

Headstones of Praying Indians
lie aslant on my father's land,
mother and son here two centuries.
Once, he took my hand and traced
the willow and urn engraved

on the flaking slabs. I'm losing
him. We both know it, though
we speak the jargon of recovery.
Now, when I gather blueberries
here by the graves, I feel

the old sting of love and heat—

not simple grief—for two
inhabitants of our sometime Eden.
Abandoned souls,
I wanted to protect them,

left berries in a mound
when I was ten, had no prayers
they'd understand, invented
chants and sang to them,
sang to the hallowed ground.

2.

The fog burns off.
The last, breath-holding days of summer,
my "gift for life" is a dim memory,
or a phrase on memory's tongue.
I've been wading through soaked grasses
to a little cemetery three hills,
three scrubby valleys away.
Here, it's always mown,
yet buggy and lonely.
I sit for hours on the damp ground,
hugging myself and deciphering
inscriptions that are eroded, moldy—

Fear, wife of Ellis
1797–18—something
Rest weary one

This must be a kind of perfection,
this proximity to distant deaths.
Before the homely histories,
I don't dwell on the shape
of anyone I love. There's nothing
under these stones, only conventions—
the faintly legible dust
of buried infants, drowned fishermen,
the long stoical lives of widows.
Because I don't want to feel
pity anymore, I study here
where the suffering's remote, antique.

3.

If I could name more constellations
would I be less afraid in the dark,
canoeing on Wakeby Lake? The islands
float like familiar spirits, sweet

and terrifying. *That small wild world* . . .
Ninety feet at its depth, the black
water could quickly take me in
if I'm at all impulsive or clumsy.

I glide uneasily, lit by a gibbous moon,
the day's deep green and dragonfly
blues burnt to charcoal, the white
line of moonlight pulling me through.

Last year, my father fished here.
From shore, I watched the slow drift
of our boat. He'd catch perch or sunnies
and throw them back and go on trolling . . .

I've brought a thermos of coffee
and muffins bleeding with berries
to comfort the chilling night.
Cancer has killed my father's appetite.

What consolation can there be in naming,
or knowing an average star dies quietly?
I've heard of the power of aging stars,
how some go on rampages, radiating

more energy than the sun. Brightest
supernovas, what do they signify?
I look up at the silent inscribed sky—
its dead lights tell a million stories.

Afterward

A week, a month, a year . . .

The rabbi's sister catalogued each stage
of mourning. Half-way through this year,
I still wake sweating to your awful pain.
Or dream you're back with us, weak but intact.

If you were to return, healthy,
a decade younger than your death age—

but those plots make my head reel,
the "ifs" that might have altered history:
"If the plot to murder Hitler had succeeded . . ."

It's only our family history you'd untrack
on its downroad, not the state of nations.

And I'd have spent the last year thinking
of you less—Cordelia, royally accused.

The few illegible notes you left—
a jumbled history—
I still would not have seen.

You never wrote me when I lived away—
that was *my* betrayal. Everyone
else you knew stayed. I fled our Freudian
romance, out until dawn with the jazz musician
you hated, then moved to another state.

More daughter than I'd have chosen,
I feared and miss your loving eye—
my late night guardian, trembling at the door.

To RTSL, 1985

"I'm drained," the last words, I think, you said
to me, four months before your death, the after-reading
crowd at Harvard lingering for a little piece of you.
Is peace to a heroic sufferer possible in the afterlife
promised by yesterday's priest at the latest funeral?
As the congregation rose, responded, and collapsed,
a crazy redhead derelict poked at my neck
with a leathery Book of Common Prayer. I deserved
it, so I didn't turn around to hiss or beg him off—
I didn't love the deceased and shuddered in failed
grief at the homily's stuffy heavenbound platitudes.

In my pew, Jewish mourners snuffled, rebuffed again
at the restricted Gates of Heaven—no everlasting
Paradise for us. Or fear of Hell. You said you wanted
words meat-hooked from the living steer. You'd miss
them in that sermon but sing a fervent Amazing Grace.
Cal, the students come, no less callow or careerist now;
their dented sensibilities might have offended
or amused you no less than Attila's or your son's
babysitter's views. Had you lived beyond that Yellow
Cab ride, you'd be nearly seventy, more frizzled,
your generation's humble chivalrous relentless pride.

Spring Planting

"This is the season
when our friends may and will die daily."
—Robert Lowell, "Soft Wood"

Last year's sunflower stalks blacken
at dusk, their huge exploded suns
droop like the heads of mourners,
frozen in sombre procession.

I carry my seedlings from the car—
snap peas, radishes, an experimental
pole bean . . .
My little green homunculi,
my hostages to a future season, you've
hardened in April's tonic breeze.

We say you'll bear in so many weeks,
that we'll be here to share the fruit—
it's easy to imagine the future wrong.

The four-year mimosa tree stands pale
and spring-naked, a body's length taller
than last year, and seems to belong.

Years back, at Temple Israel Sunday School
on Saturdays, we donated flattened one-dollar bills
for planting trees in new-born Israel.
Survivors would "make the desert bloom"—
Reform American kids helped prevent erosion.
I imagined dark enormous pines,

my father's sweet name
a plaque on one I'd never find . . .

My friend, your last days among us,
you were such a frail leaf tossing
in pain's hurricane, until morphine
finally took you to sleep with my other
lost ones in a distant forest . . .
                                        I place
the flats on the ground by a rusty trowel.
Soon, when the mimosa blossoms again,
its delicate pink blooms will sway
in the Cape's harsh wind, and drop—

oriental creature, its feathery flowers
are evanescent as the colorless smoke
your last cigarette blew across my room.